LAKOTA

Heather Bruegl

21st Century Junior Library

Indigenous Peoples of North America

Published in the United States of America by:

Cherry Lake Press
2395 South Huron Parkway, Suite 200, Ann Arbor, Michigan 48104
www.cherrylakepress.com

Reading Adviser: Beth Walker Gambro, MS, Ed., Reading Consultant, Yorkville, IL

Photo Credits: William Prokopyk/DVIDS/Public Domain, cover, title page; © AP Photo/Reed Hoffmann, 5; © imageBROKER.com GmbH & Co. KG/Alamy, 6; © AP Photo/Rapid City Journal, Steve McEnroe, 8–9; © AP Photo/Rapid City Journal. Joel Ebert, 10–11; © AFF/Alamy, 13; © Wirestock Creators/Shutterstock, 14; © Ahzoov/Wikimedia Commons via CC BY 4.0, 17; © Sebastian Kahnert/picture-alliance/dpa/AP Images, 19; © Greg Vaughn/Alamy, 21

Cherry Lake Press is an imprint of Cherry Lake Publishing Group.

Library of Congress Cataloging-in-Publication Data has been filed and is available at catalog.loc.gov

Cherry Lake Publishing Group would like to acknowledge the work of the Partnership for 21st Century Learning, a Network of Battelle for Kids. Please visit Battelle for Kids online for more information.

Printed in the United States of America

Note from publisher: Websites change regularly, and their future contents are outside of our control. Supervise children when conducting any recommended online searches for extended learning opportunities.

Cherry Lake Press

CONTENTS

WHO WE ARE

The Lakota have lived in what is now the United States for thousands of years. The word *Lakota* means "friends" or "allies" in *Lakȟótiyapi*, the Lakota language. They are one of the nations also known as the Sioux. The word *Sioux* comes from the Ojibwe word *Nadowessioux*, or "little snakes."

The Lakota Women Warriors color guard is an all-female veterans group that honors Lakota culture.

The Lakota are part of the *Oceti Sakowin*, or Seven Council Fires. The Seven Council Fires is an **alliance** between seven major nations of the Lakota, Dakota, and Nakota peoples. There are seven bands of Lakota. Each band has its own subgroups and family groups.

The four colors of the medicine wheel represent the four directions and the connection of all things.

Think!

The number seven is important to the Lakota. What evidence can you find in the text for this?

The Lakota believe in *Mitakuye Oyasin*, or "all things are connected." Everything in the universe is connected. There are seven Lakota values that the people live by. They are called the Seven **Sacred** Laws. They are fortitude, generosity, **kinship**, prayer, respect, wisdom, and compassion. These values are at the heart of what it means to be Lakota.

OUR LIVES TODAY

Today, there are seven Lakota tribes. Six of them are in the United States and one is in Canada. Around half of the Lakota population in the United States live on **reservations**. Pine Ridge is the largest of the Lakota reservations. It has 2.1 million acres (850,000 hectares) of land and is home to 40,000 people.

Clarence Wolf Guts served in World War II as a Lakota code talker.

Donald Montileaux (Oglala Lakota) brings Lakota culture to the world with his award-winning art.

Look!

What do you notice about Donald Montileaux's painting? How do you think it connects to Lakota culture?

Lakota citizens can be found in all professions across the United States and beyond. Many serve or have served in the military. Some are artists, some are lawyers, some are leaders, and some are teachers. Many work to help their nation and their people.

Dr. Tamee Livermont is a Lakota surgeon. She didn't know any Indigenous surgeons as she grew up, so she decided to become one.

Dr. Claymore Kills First is a doctor and professor. He believes Indigenous doctors are the next step of traditional Indigenous healing. He helps train new healers.

Dyani White Hawk is another Lakota artist. Her work has been shown in collections across the country. She has worked and studied in countries around the world. She says, "A driving force within what I do is about making sure that Native voices are included and heard and celebrated."

Zahn McClarnon is a Lakota actor. He has acted in TV shows and movies since the 1980s. He is proud that more Indigenous storytellers are getting the chance to tell their stories on screen. In a magazine interview, he said, "We need more Native showrunners. We need more Native executives. We need more Native producers. We're getting there, though."

Zahn McClarnon

Create!

Design your own Indigenous film festival. With an adult, go online to research a list of age-appropriate films by Indigenous producers, directors, or actors. Make a flyer advertising the festival. Include information on the creators.

The Black Hills stretch across South Dakota and Wyoming. These hills are sacred to the Lakota.

OUR ANCESTRAL LANDS

The traditional lands of the Lakota spread over a large area. They include parts of Wyoming, Montana, North Dakota, Nebraska, Colorado, and South Dakota. The center of their lands is in the Black Hills of South Dakota, where their **origin story** starts.

Lakota faith finds sacredness in all things. This includes a sacred kinship with the land. The land is alive and should be cared for as it cares for humanity.

The Lakota peoples traveled throughout their ancestral lands. They followed herds of bison, often called buffalo. The bison is a sacred animal. It provided for Lakota peoples since the beginning. It gave them food, clothing, tools, and shelter. They honor the bison and the other animals that bring them strength.

In the 1868 **Treaty** of Fort Laramie, the United States government promised to leave these lands to the Lakota. But in the mid-1870s, that promise was broken. The United States kept expanding westward. Settlers built homes and towns on Lakota land. Miners dug for gold in the Black Hills.

Ask Questions!

What questions do you have about the events after the Treaty of Fort Laramie? Make a plan to find answers.

The Crazy Horse Memorial was started in 1948 to honor the Lakota hero. It is still under construction.

The U.S. Army protected the settlers and miners. The Lakota fought back. Leaders of the Lakota resistance became legends. Sitting Bull, Crazy Horse, Red Cloud, and Black Elk all rose to fame. Their strength and wisdom helped the Lakota survive.

CARRYING TRADITIONS FORWARD

Today, people have formed movements to reclaim land that was taken from the Lakota. Many **activists** are involved in the Land Back Movement. They work to restore lands to the Lakota. They also work to rebuild the Lakota relationship with the land.

Some activists are working to protect the land from oil pipelines. These pipelines may harm the land and the water around them. The Lakota know that protecting the land and water today will help keep their people strong in the future.

Make a Guess!

What other ways do you think Lakota people work to protect the land and water? Research to find out if you were right.

Lakota peoples pass their way of life down to their children. Elders hold positions of honor. They help teach the Lakota language. They also teach traditional arts like weaving, beadwork, and porcupine quillwork.

Lakota ceremonies and sacred rites continue to guide Lakota peoples today.

GLOSSARY

activists (AK-tih-vists) people who openly take action to support a cause

alliance (uh-LIE-uhns) an agreement between groups that share certain goals and agree to work together

kinship (KIN-ship) an understanding of the importance of family relationships and one's responsibility to them

origin story (OR-uh-juhn STOR-ee) a group's story of how it came to be

reservations (reh-zer-VAY-shuhnz) legally designated plots of land held in trust for Indigenous peoples by the U.S. federal government

sacred (SAY-kruhd) holy; important to a system of belief

treaty (TREE-tee) a legal document similar to a contract that is signed between nations

FIND OUT MORE

Books

Bruegl, Heather. *What Is Land Back?* Ann Arbor, MI: Cherry Lake Publishing, 2024.

Shoulders, Michael, and Debbie Shoulders. *D is for Drum: A Native American Alphabet.* Ann Arbor, MI: Sleeping Bear Press, 2006.

Sorell, Traci. *We Are Still Here! Native American Truths Everyone Should Know.* Watertown, MA: Charlesbridge, 2021.

Online

With an adult, explore more online with these suggested searches.

- "History of the Great Lakota, Dakota, Nakota Nation," Official Website of the Traditional & Spiritual International Government of the Great Lakota, Dakota, Nakota Nation
- "Lakota Culture," Aktá Lakota Museum & Cultural Center

Say Hello!

Canté wasté nape ciyuzapo (CHAN-tay WAHSH-day nah-pay chee-yoo-zah-poh) is a Lakota greeting that means "I greet you from my heart."

INDEX

ABOUT THE AUTHOR

Heather Bruegl, a member of the Oneida Nation of Wisconsin/Stockbridge-Munsee, is a Madonna University graduate with a Master of Arts in U.S. History. She is a public historian and decolonial educator, and her Munsee name is Kiishookunkwe, meaning "Sunflower in Full Bloom." Heather frequently travels to present on Indigenous history, policy, and activism, bringing her deep knowledge and personal connection to the subject.